Great Doubt

great doubt

PRACTICING ZEN IN THE WORLD

BOSHAN

Translated and introduced by
Jeff Shore

Wisdom

Wisdom Publications
199 Elm Street
Somerville, MA 02144 USA
wisdompubs.org

Library of Congress Cataloging-in-Publication Data
Names: Yuanlai, 1575–1630, author. | Shore, Jeff, translator, writer of added
    commentary. | Yuanlai, 1575–1630. Shi yi qing fa bu qi jing yu. English. |
    Yuanlai, 1575–1630. Shi yi qing fa de qi jing yu. English.
Title: Great doubt : practicing Zen in the world / Boshan ; translated and
    introduced by Jeff Shore.
Other titles: Practicing Zen in the world
Description: Somerville, MA : Wisdom Publications, 2016. | Includes
    bibliographical references and index.
Identifiers: LCCN 2015041268 | ISBN 9781614292302 (paperback) |
    ISBN 1614292302 (paperback) | ISBN 9781614292456 (Ebook)
Subjects: LCSH: Spiritual life—Zen Buddhism. | BISAC: RELIGION /
    Buddhism /Zen (see also PHILOSOPHY / Zen). | PHILOSOPHY /
    Zen. | RELIGION / Buddhism / Sacred Writings.
Classification: LCC BQ9289 .Y78 2016 | DDC 294.3/420427—dc23
LC record available at http://lccn.loc.gov/2015041268

ISBN 978-1-61429-230-2   ebook ISBN 978-1-61429-245-6

20 19 18 17 16
5 4 3 2 1

Cover and interior design by Gopa&Ted2, Inc., typeset by LC in
Requiem 10.9/15.8.

🌸 This book was produced with environmental mindfulness.
For more information, please visit wisdompubs.org/wisdom-environment.

Printed in the United States of America.

Please visit fscus.org.

Table of Contents

Foreword

BY BRAD WARNER

Boshan's book about Great Doubt reminds me of what I found most frustrating about punk rock back when I was a faithful believer in that form of music and expression. To me punk rock wasn't an end in itself. It was an attitude that allowed you to deeply penetrate into the truth of everything. We were on a quest to find the reality behind the facade presented to us by the corporate-controlled media. We were all about questioning everything, including ourselves. Or so I thought.

But lots of people started coming in to the scene for whom punk rock was nothing more than a set of very specific fashion choices and an exceedingly limited way of musical expression. They didn't see that punk rock was also about Great Doubt.

One of the first things I ever heard about Zen practice from my first Zen teacher was that it requires equal amounts of doubt and faith. This was both a shock and a great relief.

At the time I was searching for something to believe in. I'd been raised without a religion and I wanted one.

I had hoped punk could be my religion, but that didn't work out. And no actual religion I encountered made any better sense either. They all insisted on faith alone. I was supposed to have faith that Jesus died for my sins, or that Krishna could have sex with a thousand cowgirls in one night, or that Moses parted the Red Sea, or any number of other things that I found myself unable to have faith in. When I heard that Zen valued doubt as much as faith I saw that here at last was something I could believe in.

In this brief but remarkably thorough book, Boshan attempts to put into words what it means to truly doubt. Not just to be skeptical—though I think skepticism is an ingredient of Great Doubt—but to push all the way to the very foundations.

Another name for Great Doubt might be Great Wonder. Perhaps wonder is the brighter aspect of doubt.

Our brains have evolved to seek certainty. In order to survive, we have to be certain about what's a snake and what's a piece of rope, which mushrooms will provide us with vitamin D and riboflavin and which will kill us, who is our true friend and who is trying to cheat us. Religions take this sensible desire for situational certainty and create the fiction of ultimate all-encompassing absolute certainty. Meditation is often expected to lead us to a state of complete and utter certainty, a state beyond all doubt.

But in this book, Boshan tells us again and again that any state that seems like ultimate certainty is just the product of our own imagination. When we lose our capacity to doubt, we lose the truth. When you remove all doubt, you also remove all wonder.

There are passages in Boshan's writing that might leave contemporary readers scratching their heads. I must admit there are a couple of times he loses me. But if you find yourself a little lost, my advice is to try not to worry so much about the particulars of what he's saying and concentrate on the attitude he is trying to convey. Because he's not trying to impart any specific information. Rather, he's trying to get us to understand the attitude he calls Great Doubt.

In *Fukan Zazengi* Dogen says, "Proud of our understanding and richly endowed with realization, we obtain special states of insight; we attain the truth; we clarify the mind; we acquire the zeal that pierces the sky; we ramble through remote intellectual spheres, going in with the head; and yet, we have almost completely lost the vigorous road of getting the body out."

Boshan never quotes this passage from Dogen. He probably never even read it. But to me he seems to be taking this very same attitude and penetrating into it as far as he can possibly go. Even in moments of the deepest and most profound insight, we need to maintain a sense of doubt, a sense of wonder.

If all you come away with after reading *Great Doubt*

is a little of Boshan's attitude, then you're a long way past the vast majority of folks who like to tell all their friends they're "into Zen" and show off all the great wisdom they possess by virtue of having once downloaded a podcast about meditation.

Boshan is writing both for beginners and for experienced practitioners. Beginners in meditation practice can often feel frustrated because they get distracted easily and meditation doesn't feel like they imagine it should. But thinking your meditation is going wrong because you have distracting thoughts is like thinking your workout is going wrong because you sweat.

Still, it's difficult. I get it. I've been there. Remembering that doubt is part of the process can make it easier to get through the rough patches. That feeling of doubt you have that you can even do this thing at all doesn't mean you're doing your meditation wrong. It means you're doing it right.

As you continue your practice, though, you'll eventually have moments where it seems like you've broken through, like you've solved every philosophical question that has bedeviled mankind for the past ten thousand centuries. You'll want to shout your new discoveries from the rooftops and lead your fellow humans into the shining New Age of peace, love, and unlimited joy that you know are the birthright of every living creature.

To people at this stage, Boshan says, "Check yourself." You may indeed have discovered something very deep, very profound. But you haven't gone all the way because you can never go all the way. Nobody can. Realize that the all-encompassing bliss you feel is just as fleeting as everything else and that reality is much bigger than you could ever imagine.

I think anyone interested in Zen can learn a whole lot from this little book.

Introduction
DOUBT IN THE ZEN TRADITION

Like other religions, Zen Buddhism encourages faith or trust—but it also encourages doubt. There are, however, two kinds of doubt: skeptical doubt and great doubt. Skeptical doubt is of little value. Indeed—along with greed, hatred, ignorance, and pride—skeptical doubt is usually considered a defilement, a hindrance, or a poison. That kind of doubt gives rise to a hesitant attitude that keeps one from entering the Way. Great doubt, the kind of doubt that Zen values, is something entirely other. There is good reason that it is called great doubt.

Great doubt is an intense wonder, a powerful curiosity that opens us up. It does not stand in opposition to trust in the Way. In fact, great doubt can arise only from great trust. Great trust grounds and supports us; great doubt keeps us on the path, and leads us all the way through. Great trust is the conviction, based on experience, that there is a way; great doubt provides the fuel to go all the way. As quoted in the sixteenth-century compendium, *Whips Through the Zen Barrier* by Zhuhong, the fourteenth-century Chinese Zen master

Zhen summed it up when he began a Dharma talk with this: "Fully trust, you'll fully doubt; fully doubt, you'll fully awaken."

Consider the life of the Buddha—his great renunciation and home-leaving, his struggle and awakening. Through it all, his quest to resolve great doubt is unmistakable. Great doubt requires our urgent attention.

In this small book, we will explore two short texts on great doubt authored by Boshan (1575–1630), one of the leading Chinese masters of the Ming dynasty. The texts are called *Exhortations for Those Who Don't Rouse Doubt* and *Exhortations for Those Who Rouse Doubt*. Boshan, or Mount Bo, is the name of the mountain where he was active; like many masters, he became known as such. He is also known as Wuyi Yuanlai and Dayi.

Boshan hailed from Shucheng in present-day Anhui Province, west of Nanjing. He left home in his midteens, took up Buddhist study and practice, including five years of sustained meditative discipline, and received full ordination. Later he practiced under the Caodong (Japanese: Sōtō) master Wuming Huijing (1548–1618), a severe teacher who persistently rejected Boshan's intial insights. One day, while sitting intently in meditation on a rock, Boshan had a sudden realization when he heard a statue nearby fall with a crash. The following year he was greatly awakened when watching a person climb a tree. He was in his late twenties at the time. Boshan received the bodhisattva precepts before teaching at several monasteries, finally settling at Mount Bo in present-day Jiangxi Province, south of Anhui. He was one of Wuming Huijing's four Dharma heirs, and he himself left behind several Dharma heirs and lay disciples. He passed away in 1630.

One of his lay disciples wrote a preface dated 1611— Boshan would have been around thirty-six years old at the time—for the larger work of which these exhortations form one part. There it states it is "truly a lifeboat for this degenerate age, a direct path for beginner's mind. Surely beneficial in the present day, it will be a great aid in the future as well."

Chinese, Korean, and Japanese editions have since been published. Boshan was prolific; in his own introduction to the larger work, which includes these two texts, Boshan emphasizes the importance of this great doubt:

> In Zen practice, the essential point is to rouse doubt. What is this doubt? When you are born, for example, where do you come from? You cannot help but remain in doubt about this. When you die, where do you go? Again, you cannot help but remain in doubt. Since you cannot pierce this barrier of life and death, suddenly doubt will coalesce right before your eyes. Try to put it down, you cannot; try to push it away, you cannot

Eventually you will break through this doubt block and realize what a worthless notion life and death is—ha! As the old worthies said: "Great doubt, great awakening; small doubt, small awakening; no doubt, no awakening."

If doubt could be avoided, trust alone would be enough. Entrusting fully is a full and complete path. For most of us, however, doubt cannot be avoided. Our very selves are split, within and without. To put it bluntly, this split itself is us. Self comes into being split: with faith and with doubt.

The late thirteenth-century Chinese Zen layman Tian also comments on the relationship between faith and doubt, as quoted in *Whips Through the Zen Barrier*:

> If trust is firm, doubt will be firm; once doubt is firm, torpor and mental scattering will naturally vanish.

Great faith and great doubt are the foundation of Zen practice, and of the distinctive character of Zen Buddhism. Boshan puts it bluntly: "In Zen practice, the essential point is to rouse doubt." The Zen Buddhist approach is: "So, you have doubt? Then doubt away—take that doubt all the way!" Practicing great doubt in this way is the consummate function of great trust.

The Edo period Japanese Zen master Hakuin put it clearly:

> To all intents and purposes, Zen practice makes as its essential the resolution of the doubt block. Thus it is said, "At the bottom of great doubt lies great awakening. If you doubt fully you will awaken fully."[1]

Yet such great doubt cannot be forced. It must arise naturally, based on a clear recognition of the great matter of life and death. Consider this exchange between the seventeenth-century Japanese Zen master Bankei and a student:

> Monk: Zen masters of old have said that great awakening proceeds from great doubt. You don't use this great doubt in your teaching. Why?
>
> Bankei: Long ago, when Nanyue went to the sixth patriarch and was asked "What is it that's thus come?" he was totally bewildered. His doubt about it lasted for eight long years. Finally he was able to respond, "Whatever I say would miss the mark." Now that's really great doubt and great awakening!
>
> Suppose you lost your only surplice, the one you were given when you became a

monk, and you were unable to find it no matter how hard you looked. You'd search and search without let-up. You'd be unable to stop searching for even an instant. That would be real doubt!

People nowadays say they need to have doubt because people in the past did. So they cultivate a doubt. But that's merely an imitation of a doubt, not a real one, so the day never comes when they arrive at a real resolution.

It's as if you were to go off looking for something you hadn't really lost, pretending you had.[2]

Make no mistake, Bankei is not criticizing great doubt; he was spurred on by great doubt since childhood. He is criticizing unnatural, forced, contrived, or made up doubt based on someone else's words or experience. Great doubt is essential.

Moreover, without great doubt, Zen practice stagnates and various problems arise—as we will see in Boshan's *Exhortations for Those Who Don't Rouse Doubt.* If we do not allow great doubt to arise, Zen practice sinks into a kind of sickness. Without great doubt our practice becomes an escape into calm and clear states of mind, insights, or so-called enlightenment experiences that the self assumes will solve all its problems.

All the while, our fundamental self-delusion is left untouched. Such practice is a big problem and, as we will see, Boshan nails it down in no uncertain terms.

Don't waste time thinking, "Maybe I don't have the right kind of doubt. I need more doubt. I need that person's doubt." There are as many entrances to great doubt as there are people. We must each find our own entrance into our own doubt.

To find that entrance, all we need to do is directly inquire into what's right under our own feet, so to speak, at the heart of it all. What's really here? Realizing this and settling into it in a sustained way is what Zen meditation, *zazen*, is all about. Genuine Zen practice naturally rouses, fosters, and encourages great doubt and helps us pour ourselves completely into it so that we can truly resolve it once and for all. Here is the great matter of life and death: the only real koan.

A traditional Zen koan asks, "What is your original face before your parents were born?" Another says, "All things return to one; where does this one return to?" The point of such questions, regardless of what form they take, is that they come to encompass everything—beginning with oneself.

Inquire with your whole being: Who is this? What is this? The Hindu sage Ramana Maharshi used the question "Who am I?" Boshan asks us, "Who comes into being at birth, and who dies at death?" Even more urgently: Who is it that reads these words right now?

Who is behind this experience? Have you really seen who is behind it all?

Great doubt can take many forms. It may first arise as a kind of intuition that comes down to the fact that I don't know who I am, where I come from, what is real. Or it may first arise as a deep-seated sensation, emotion, or feeling of dis-ease, a sense that I'm not at peace, I cannot come fully to rest with myself or with others; a deeply felt inchoate awareness something's not right. Or it may first arise as a problem of will or volition, a sense that, no matter what, I can't seem to get free, as if I'm banging up against the wall of my own self; however much I try to do what is good and right, I fail.

If doubt first arises as a feeling that you are not at peace, then inquire directly into who it is that is not at peace. If doubt first arises as a problem of will, look into the early Zen ancestor Shitou's challenge: "As-you-are will not do; not-as-you-are will not do. Either way, nothing will do. Now what?"

In whatever way doubt arises, it's essential that we properly direct and focus it. On this point, the twelfth-century Chinese master Dahui and others speak of "a thousand doubts, ten thousand doubts— just one doubt." Without such focus, while doubt may be clear and substantial at first, it will then fade again into the background and never be fully resolved. Thus many people attempt meditation for some time, then grow disillusioned with it and give up. Failing to penetrate the surface, they are honest enough to recognize that their minds are still going in the same old circles.

Great doubt cannot be a mere object of awareness—it is much more real and immediate than that. When one truly practices with great doubt, doubt becomes the essential koan. In fact, koans and doubt are not two separate things. Consider this teaching from Chinese master Deng's "Compendium on Resolving Doubt," quoted in *Whips Through the Zen Barrier*:

> Question: Practicing under teachers, some of them say to focus on the koan and some say to doubt the koan. Are these the same or different?
>
> Answer: As soon as you focus on the koan, doubt arises—why separate them? Focus on the koan and doubt will immediately arise. Continue investigating, and when your efforts reach their limit, you'll naturally awaken.

This doubt is essential, as we can see in the following quotations, first from the Chinese master Gaofeng Yuanmiao of the thirteenth century, second from Zongbao, one of Boshan's Dharma heirs, and third from Hakuin:

In India and China, in the past and the present, of all the worthies who spread this light, none did anything more than simply resolve this one doubt. The thousand doubts, the ten thousand doubts are just this one doubt. Resolve this doubt and no doubt remains.[3]

This doubt is another name for what is most pressing and urgent. Once you acknowledge this pressing and urgent matter of life and death as your own, the doubt will arise of its own accord. If you continue to doubt, then quite naturally the time and conditions will arrive. If you idle away your time without making efforts and merely wait for enlightenment, the day will never come.

It is all a matter of raising or failing to raise this doubt block. It must be understood that this doubt block is like a pair of wings that advances you along the way.[4]

Chinul, founder of the Korean Zen tradition, followed the lead of Chinese master Dahui, who was renowned for developing introspection on, or boring into, the koan to rouse great doubt. Great doubt continues to play a central role in Korean Zen today, as it does in China and Japan. And this is true not simply in the Rinzai tradition; Boshan himself, who authored *Exhortations*, was a master in the Sōtō (Chinese: Caodong) tradition.

Rousing great doubt might seem suitable only for monastics devoting their lives to the Way. This is another common misconception to dispel. Dahui went so far as to say in a letter to one of his many experienced lay disciples: "When has it ever been necessary to leave wife and children, quit one's job, and chew on vegetable roots, thus hurting the body and weakening the spirit?" Dahui goes on to say that home-leavers, that is, monks like himself, "are on the outside breaking in; laypeople (like you) are on the inside breaking out. The power of one on the outside breaking in is weak; the power of one on the inside breaking out is strong."[5]

When great doubt reaches its critical stage, proper guidance by one who has actually been through it is most valuable, as Boshan and others repeatedly state. At the same time, established in proper practice while living in the world, with all its temptations and confusions, we are right where we need to be to bring the practice to life rather than use it as an escape.

My task here is to introduce and comment on Boshan's *Exhortations* as living words relevant for us today. Despite the many false starts koan Zen has had in the West, experienced Dharma friends around the globe are now coming together for sustained practice, proving what Dahui stated above. It will be a great joy if this small book can play a small part in seeing it through.

translation

Exhortations for Those
Who Don't Rouse Doubt

If you're unable to rouse doubt when practicing Zen, you may seek intellectual understanding through the written word. Stringing together with a single thread the various phrases and teachings of buddhas and patriarchs, you stamp them all with one seal. If a koan is brought up, you are quick to give your interpretation. Unable to rouse your own doubt concerning the koan, you don't like it when someone probes you with serious questions. All this is simply your wavering mind; it is not Zen.

You may respond at once to questions by raising a finger or showing a fist. Taking up an ink brush, you promptly pen a verse to show off, hoping to guide unwitting students to your level. Fascinated with all this, you refer to it as the gate of enlightenment. You don't realize that such karmic consciousness is precisely what prevents this doubt from arising. If only you would straight off see the error of your ways, then you should once and for all let go of all and seek out a good teacher or Dharma friend to help you find an entrance. If not, your wavering mind will prevail, you'll become as if demon-possessed, and release will be very difficult.

THE DISEASE OF QUIET MEDITATION

If you're unable to rouse doubt when practicing Zen, you may develop an aversion to the world of conditions. Thus, you escape to a quiet place and sink into zazen meditation. Empowered by this, you find it quite fascinating. When you have to get up and do something, however, you dislike it. This too is simply your wavering mind; it is not Zen.

Sitting long in zazen, sunk in quietness; within this mystic darkness the senses fuse, objects and opposition disappear. But even if you enter dhyāna absorption without mind movement, it's no different from the Hinayana. Any contact with the world and you feel uneasy with your loss of freedom: hearing sounds or seeing sights, you're gripped by fear. Frightened, you become as if demon-possessed and commit evil acts. In the end, you waste a lifetime of practice in vain. All because from the first, you failed to rouse this doubt—thus, you did not seek out a true guide or trust one. Instead, you stubbornly sit self-satisfied in your quiet hole. Even if you meet a good teacher or Dharma friend, if you don't immediately recognize your error, innumerable buddhas may appear and preach the Dharma but they won't be able to save you.

THE DISEASE OF SUPPRESSION

If you're unable to rouse doubt when practicing Zen, you may suppress emotions and discriminating consciousness so that no delusions can arise, then dwell in this apparently calm and lucid state. But you fail to thoroughly break through the root source of consciousness and instead dwell on its immaculateness. Even though you may practice and understand everything from within this apparently pure and lucid state, once you encounter someone who points out your failure, then emotions and discriminating consciousness pop up like a gourd that was pushed under water. This too is simply your wavering mind; it is not Zen.

And all because from the time you first took up a koan you failed to rouse this doubt. Even if you could suppress all delusions so that they no longer arise, it would be like trying to press down the grass with a stone—delusions will just grow around it. And if you fail to do so, when in contact with the world of conditions, karmic consciousness will be stirred up. Even if you do actually cut off and put a stop to all karmic consciousness, that is falling into the heretical path of dead emptiness. Then in the immaculate state that is produced, you convince yourself you've attained sainthood or enlightenment. Continue in this way and you will become arrogant; attached to this state, you will become as if demon-possessed. Entangled in the world and deluding others with your ignorance, you end up committing serious offenses, betraying the trust others have in the Dharma, and obstructing the path of awakening.

THE DISEASE OF EMPTINESS

If you're unable to rouse doubt when practicing Zen, you may come to regard the physical and mental worlds as utterly emptied, with nothing at all to cling to and nothing to hold on to. Unable to discern your own body and mind or the world around you, denying inner and outer, you make everything into one emptiness. Then you believe this emptying to be Zen, and the one who emptied it all to be a buddha. You imagine that the four postures of going, staying, sitting, and reclining are done within emptiness. This too is simply your wavering mind; it is not Zen.

Continuing in this way you end up in false emptiness, sunk in dark ignorance. Attached to it, you become as if demon-possessed and proclaim that you've attained enlightenment. All because you fail to realize that what you're doing has nothing to do with true Zen inquiry. If you genuinely inquire, with one koan you'd rouse this doubt and wield it as a razor sharp sword—whoever comes in contact with its blade will be annihilated. Otherwise, even though you may reach a state of emptiness where no thoughts arise, it is still ignorance and far from final.

THE DISEASE OF SPECULATION

If you're unable to rouse doubt when practicing Zen, you may end up speculating with your karmic consciousness over the koans of old, sloppily scratching the surface. Then you declare it to be the whole truth, or at least half, as absolute, as relative, this as lord and that as vassal, unity attained, clear and simple words, and so on, all the while praising yourself for your superior understanding. Even if you could interpret and explain away each and every one, spewing out the words of old as your own, this too is simply your wavering mind; it is not Zen.

You don't realize that you're merely taking the words and phrases of old and chewing them like balled-up cotton thread, unable to either swallow them or spit them out. How can such things create paths of liberation for others? How can they lead others to genuine insight? On the other hand, if you rouse this doubt and throw yourself into it, then without waiting until the end of your life, karmic consciousness will cease of its own accord and entangling interpretations will naturally be put to rest.

THE DISEASE OF SPIRITS

If you're unable to rouse doubt when practicing Zen, you may conclude: "Body and mind are dependent on the confluence of fleeting conditions. However, within all of this, there is one thing that comes and goes, free in both motion and rest, without form or substance, shining from the sense organs. Spread out, it fills the universe; gathered in, not a dust mote remains!" With such an understanding, you fail to even try and rouse this doubt or to truly inquire, presuming instead that you have completed the great matter. This too is simply your wavering mind; it is not Zen.

You fail to realize that what you are doing is not breaking through the samsaric mind of life and death at all, but instead delighting in such understanding—self-deluded playing with spirits. When the last light of your eyes falls to the ground and death comes, you'll lose your precious hold. Then you'll be dragged about by your so-called spirits and have to repay your karmic debts. If you're able to accrue plenty of good karma, you may be reborn into the realm of humans or gods. Then facing death again, you'll find yourself crying:

"The Buddhadharma has no saving power!" Slandering the Buddhadharma like this, you'll fall into the hell of hungry ghosts—and heaven knows how long you'll take to get out of that. You'd better find a true Dharma friend and inquire into this with them, for your complacent spirit will be of no help here.

THE DISEASE OF ACTING OUT

If you're unable to rouse doubt when practicing Zen, you may think: "Eyes see, ears hear, the tongue speaks, the nose smells odors, hands grasp, feet run. All this is the true nature of the spiritual self!" You then conclude that you're enlightened and go about eyeballing people, bending an ear, pointing at this and kicking at that, thinking it's all the personification of Buddhadharma. But this too is simply your wavering mind; it is not Zen.

Of old, such nonsense has been compared to temporary insanity, or likened to sitting in the master's formal chair with a frightening scowl frozen on your face. What good will all that do when you're facing death? Even worse are those who transmit this stuff to the next generation and accept offerings from the faithful without the least bit of shame. If someone asks about the Dharma, they yell or let out a big laugh. They have never truly inquired themselves, so they cannot cut through their samsaric life root. In such a situation, even countless good deeds become the handiwork of the devil. And all because they fail to recognize that where they have reached is far from final.

THE DISEASE OF ASCETICISM

If you're unable to rouse doubt when practicing Zen, you may become obsessed with a goal, preoccupied with achieving liberation, or even undergo ascetic extremes. You won't seek warmth in winter or shade in summer. Asked for a piece of clothing, you give away your whole wardrobe. Content with freezing to death, you assume it to be liberation. Asked for food, you go without eating. Content with starving to death, you assume it to be liberation. It takes many forms but, generally speaking, comes from an intention to achieve and conquer. Thus you end up deceiving the unwitting, who take you for a living buddha or bodhisattva and give all they can as offerings. People don't realize that this is abusing the Buddhist precepts and that all such acts are harmful.

Others, as Dharma practice, burn part of their bodies in sacrificial offerings, constantly worship the Buddha, and confess their faults. From the worldly viewpoint, this is certainly virtuous. As far as true inquiry goes, however, it is quite meaningless. As has been said since of old: "Never get attached to Dharma expressions." Worshipping the Buddha is one such Dharma expression, as is confession. All good things of the Buddhadharma are so. I am not saying to dispense with them but to do them with singleness of mind, thus to nourish the roots of all that is good. When your Dharma eye opens, you will see: sweeping away the burnt incense offerings is itself Buddha work.

THE DISEASE OF SELF-INDULGENCE

If you're unable to rouse doubt when practicing Zen, you may fall into self-indulgent and wild ways. Meeting others, you sing, dance, and carry on. By the river and under trees you recite poetry, prattle, and laugh. Swaggering about busy places regardless of others, you convince yourself that you've resolved the great matter. When you see a worthy teacher open a meditation hall, establish rules for the sangha, do zazen, chant the name of the Buddha, and do other virtuous acts, you let out a scornful laugh and curse him. Since you're not able to truly practice, you disturb others who are. Not knowing how to truly recite the sutras, worship, or confess your faults, you hinder others who do. Unable to truly inquire, you interrupt those who do. You can't open your own meditation hall, so you interfere with those who have. Unable to give a real Dharma talk, you interrupt those who do. Seeing a worthy teacher present a Dharma talk in front of a large congregation, you think up complicated questions and indulge in silly exchanges, giving a Zen shout or a slap. The worthy teacher recognizes such things as no more than ghostly spirits playing games. If he does not indulge you, however, you spread groundless rumors: "He doesn't understand the Dharma principle—what a pity!"

This is your wavering mind obsessed; if you continue this way, you will fall into demonic paths and commit serious offenses. Once your good karma is exhausted, you'll fall into the hell of incessant suffering. "Even good intentions have bad results." Alas!

THE DISEASE OF PUTTING ON AIRS

If you're unable to rouse doubt when practicing Zen, you may feel annoyed by the restrictions of the sangha. Some may want to go deep in the mountains where there's no one around. For a while they may be satisfied there, closing eyes and unifying mind with legs in full lotus and hands in grateful prayer. After a few months or years, however, they find themselves lost. Others, after sitting only a few days, turn to reading books and composing poetry. Self-indulgent, they shut the door and doze off. From a distance they seem dignified, but up close their decadence knows no bounds. Others are like juvenile delinquents greedily sneaking around, neither knowing shame nor fearing karmic retribution. Putting on airs and speaking as if they knew, they deceive the unwitting: "I met a great teacher! He transmitted the Dharma to me!" and so on. They herd the unwitting into their flock, then keep company with them or even make them their disciples. They act Zen-like and those under them follow suit. Unaware of their errors, they do not even know to reflect on themselves or feel regret, to seek out a worthy teacher or Dharma friend. Reckless and arrogant, they spread terrible lies. They are really pitiful. Recently, some have grown weary of the sangha and now seek out their own living quarters. It should send shivers up their spines!

If you are to genuinely seek the Way, I trust you'll drop such notions. Then you can inquire together with others in the sangha, and work together to keep an eye on things. Even if you cannot realize the Way, at least you will not fall into such corrupt paths. Practicing the Way, you must beware of these dangers.

Exhortations for Those Who Rouse Doubt

Rousing doubt when practicing Zen, one accords with dharmakāya. Then the whole world is radiant, without the slightest hindrance.

But then you try to take control and can't let it go. Clinging to it like this, the life root cannot be cut off. Thinking you know the dharmakāya and acting as if you fully understood it and were benefiting from it, in fact these are all your delusions. The ancients have warned that in true intimacy, words can separate. Because the life root has not been cut off, you're sick through and through. This is not Zen.

Here you must submit yourself completely and accept whatever comes, without even knowing who does what. As an ancient worthy said:

> Let go on the edge of the precipice and
>   accept what comes!
> Finish dying, then come back to life and
>   you can no longer be deceived.

If the life root is not cut off, your arising, ceasing mind will just continue in samsaric circles. And even though it is cut off, if you don't realize the needed turnaround you'll be as if dwelling with the dead, for you have yet to reach the end.

It's not difficult to realize; the problem lies with your refusing to encounter good Dharma friends and teachers. If you did, with one thrust to your weak point you'd directly realize it. Otherwise, you'll be just a living corpse!

Rousing doubt when practicing Zen, one accords with dharmakāya. Then one seems able to draw the world into a vortex and rouse enormous waves at will.

But the practitioner gets attached to this and will not budge however much he is pushed or pulled. Thus he cannot throw himself fully into the real work. Like a penniless person coming upon a mountain of gold, he knows full well it's gold but can't make use of it. This the ancients decried as a greedy treasure guard. Such a person is sick through and through. This is not Zen.

In this state, just throw yourself into it with no regard for danger. Only then will you come to accord with Dharma. As Master Tiantong said: "The vast Dharma world then becomes like so much cooked rice: whatever your nose falls upon, your belly feels full!" Otherwise, you're like someone starving to death next to the rice bucket, or dying of thirst while surrounded by water. What good does that do?

Thus it is said: "After satori, you must go and see someone worthy," just as the ancients went to see good teachers and Dharma friends after their satori and benefited greatly from doing so. If you adamantly cling to your present practice and refuse to visit those who can remove the needle in your eye and the wedge in your head, you're a fool who deceives himself!

Rousing doubt when practicing Zen, one accords with dharmakāya. Then you see that mountains are not mountains, rivers are not rivers, and the whole world is one, solid (doubt block) without the slightest gap.

As soon as discursive mind returns, however, your vision is obstructed and you feel hindered in body and mind. You can neither raise up great doubt nor break through it. And if you can raise it up for a while it may seem to be there, but when you let go it's gone. You open your mouth yet you cannot exhale, nor can you move freely or change your pace. Either way, you don't get it. At such a point you're sick through and through, this is not Zen.

Because the ancients were pure and simple in heart, without discursive mind or second thoughts, they could rouse doubt to the point where mountains were not mountains and rivers were no longer rivers. Thus their doubt block was suddenly broken through and their whole body became the single eye. Then the mountains and rivers are, for the first time, seen as the mountains and rivers that they always were—one realizes where mountains, rivers, and the great earth really come from. Here there's not the slightest trace of satori.

Precisely here you need to seek out someone who knows. Otherwise, you'll be lost as if in an endless terrain of dead trees with ever-diverging paths. Whoever continues right on through here, without tripping over the roots and branches, I (Boshan) want to be a Dharma friend with him!

Rousing doubt when practicing Zen, one accords with dharmakāya. But then you fall into blank stillness where nothing arises, as if experiencing ten thousand years in one moment of thought. Thus your sensation of doubt gets stubbornly stuck in the abstract notion of dharmakāya so it can't spring to life and function freely. Lifeless and unresponsive, lacking the transformative turn, indecisive and without vitality, as if sunk in stagnant water. Yet you mistakenly take this state for the ultimate. Sick through and through, this is not Zen.

There were plenty like this in Shishuang's congregation. Even if they die seated in meditation or while standing, they can't spring to life and function freely. If an able teacher took up his forging tools, the sincere among them would get the point, turn round, and breathe free. Then they'd be really human!

If not, even though they understand the words and cut off the ten directions in sitting, what good will it do? As Tiantong said: "Just cutting off the ten directions in sitting, the fish falls short of the Dragon Gate. Leap through and see—the dragon soars up to the heavens!"

Since days of old there have been many exhortations to guide us, and plenty of records to instruct us. This is because practitioners don't go all the way but instead seek to imitate their teachers moving freely among the chaotic crowd. No wonder they have a hard time.

Rousing doubt when practicing Zen, one accords with dharmakāya. In zazen the point is reached where nothing disturbs, and one feels completely naked and free—beyond grasping.

But then you get stuck there, not knowing how to change freely with time and conditions. Attached to this state, you dare to act as lord and master, stagnating in (what you take to be) dharmakāya. Sick through and through, this is not Zen.

Dongshan Liangjie said:

> Mountain summit soars, but the crane does
>   not abide.
> The tree is lofty, but the phoenix does not
>   reside.

Soaring summits and lofty trees refer to something extremely subtle and profound. They are not merely dry, lifeless expressions. Likewise, not abiding and not residing refer to something extremely energetic and full of life, rather than something stagnant and still.

If not penetrated to this depth, the profound Dharma principle won't be known. And if this liveliness is not reached, the constantly free and marvelous dynamism has not been realized.

One committed to the practice exhausts his mind to the very limit. Then, through encountering a genuine teacher, the bucket of lacquer is overturned and one can see through. How can you foolishly hold on to your ignorance and remain satisfied like a crane in its cage or a phoenix shedding its feathers?

Rousing doubt when practicing Zen, one accords with dharmakaya. Then, although unclear, something seems to arise in front of you. Groping after this vague something time and again, it eventually appears right before your very eyes. You then convince yourself that you have grasped the truth of dharmakāya and realized the true nature of the universe. You don't know that such things are mere fantasies and illusions. Sick through and through, this is not Zen.

If someone has really penetrated this truth, it's a matter of "the world widening to ten feet is the ancient mind mirror widening to ten feet." Since "stretching out your body is the spread of the universe," there is not a thing to seek within or without. What on earth do you take to be your body, to be facing you, to exist— what is that vague something?

Unmon Bun'en also pointed out this sickness and spoke much of it. If one can clearly see through this sickness, then all three sicknesses will completely dissolve. I have spoken of this to my students: "Innumerable sicknesses are found in the dharmakāya. Fatally succumb once to this—only then will you realize the root of the disease. Even if everyone over the face of the earth practiced Zen, not one of them would be spared from this sickness." This does not, of course, apply to the blind, deaf, and dumb.

Rousing doubt when practicing Zen, one accords with dharmakaya. This is what men of old called "the whole world is the monk's eye," "the whole world is one's luminosity," "the whole world is within one's luminosity." As the sutras speak of it, "within one speck of dust there are infinite Dharma truths."

But then you grasp that as final and don't proceed further or with proper guidance. Convincing yourself that this is an entrance gate into satori, you fall into a state where you're not really living nor are you finished dying. Sick through and through, this is not Zen.

Even though you reach accord with dharmakāya, you don't realize that if you can't get free from it you end up falling under its spell. Even worse if you turn it into something and get dragged down by it; unable to fully penetrate, the monkey mind can't stop grasping after it. Thus you can't finish dying—how on earth can you come back to life?

Begin by rousing doubt, and then accord with dharmakāya. According with dharmakāya, plumb its depths. Then turn somersaults on the edge of a precipice. Back on solid ground, you wave to others and sail downstream as if nothing happened. Only then will you be worthy of guiding others. Otherwise, you're but a fraud scratching the surface, not Buddha's true successor.

Rousing doubt when practicing Zen, one accords with dharmakāya. Whether going, staying, sitting, or reclining, it feels like basking in sunlight or being enveloped in the soft glow of a lamp, serenely undisturbed. If you proceed from there and let go of that, it's like the refreshing breeze in the moonlight by a clear lake. Your own body and the whole world are completely one, all utterly pure, senses clear and sharp. Now you're really convinced that this is the ultimate!

But you can't turn round and take that further step, nor can you return to the world with open arms to help others. You don't even consider consulting with Dharma friends or teachers whether this is really the ultimate or not. In this state of purity you rouse delusions, then assume you have entered the gate of satori. Sick through and through, this is not Zen.

Tiantong said:

> Even though the moon shines bright, you
>   lose your way home;

There's no room to doubt, yet try to step
forward and you fall.

"Even though the moon shines bright" clearly is none other than "the refreshing breeze in the moonlight by a clear lake." "There's no room to doubt," yet even if you step forward you end up "losing your way" and "fall."

What should practitioners do when they get to this point? Simply and easily turn and be transformed from a single blade of grass into a ten-foot-tall golden buddha. Otherwise, it will be like trying to row a boat by hammering down the oars, or trying to catch fish up a tree. Destroy a thousand or a million of their ilk, still you'll commit no crime.

Rousing doubt when practicing Zen, one accords with dharmakāya. But the moment you distort the dharmakāya by creating magical and marvelous delusions, then shining lights, flowers, and all sorts of esoteric manifestations appear. You then think you've achieved the ultimate and, convinced that you've entered the gate of satori, bedazzle and deceive others with what you've seen. You don't realize that actually you're sick through and through and that this is not Zen.

You should know that these strange visions are fixations of your own delusions, like things conjured up in your mind by demons, or temptations by heavenly beings such as Indra. For example, such delusive visions are found in the sixteen contemplations of *The Sutra on Contemplation of Immeasurable Life*. By devoting oneself to being reborn in the Pure Land, all of a sudden images of buddhas and bodhisattvas appear, and this is in accord with Pure Land doctrine. But it is not the way of Zen.

The *Surangama Sutra* mentions this conjuring by demons: when realizing the emptiness of the five aggregates, if there is still some attachment in the mind, demons will immediately appear. The temptations by heavenly beings refer for example to Indra transforming into headless demons and the like to scare the practicing bodhisattva, but he is not frightened. Then Indra transforms into a beautiful woman to entice the practitioner, but he remains unmoved by desire. Finally Indra appears undisguised and bows, saying: "The great Mount Tai may crumble and the vast ocean dry up, but it is truly difficult to move his mind!" Thus it is said: "There's a limit to a worldly man's tricks, but no end to this old monk's not seeing and not hearing."

If you are really intent on pursuing this path, even if a murderer wields his knife in front of your face, you won't bat an eyelash. Deep in meditation, you certainly won't be bothered by illusions. One with the Dharma principle, there is nothing outside the mind. Where is there room for the seeing mind and what is seen?

Rousing doubt when practicing Zen, one accords with dharmakāya. Then one feels lightness in body and mind, and no hindrance in any situation. But even if one experiences the unity of reality and appearance, and the whole world seems in harmony for the moment, it is not the ultimate. This is where the ignorant, convinced that they've entered the gate of satori, are quick to let go of their doubt and proceed no further. Because the life root has not been cut off, they don't realize that even though they may have approached the Dharma, all is still within the realm of karmic consciousness. Speculating with their karmic consciousness, they are sick through and through. This is not Zen.

Without penetrating the Dharma, they have turned round too soon. Thus, even though they may understand deeply, they cannot bring it to life. If only they truly turned round with a living word—then they could patiently cultivate and mature along the riverbank or in forests. Never be in a rush to save others while pride and conceit remain.

Beginning the practice, take great care to rouse

this doubt so that it solidifies into one massive block. When this breaks up on its own, the real one bursts forth and comes to life. Otherwise, you only approach the Dharma and thus prematurely let go of your doubt. You'll never finish dying that way, nor will you thoroughly penetrate. Instead you will waste your life in vain. Even if you continue to practice Zen, it will be in name only and not the real thing. Intending to return to the world with open arms to help others—you better encounter a true teacher or real Dharma friend instead. Such ones are great doctors who can help heal fatal ills and offer whatever is really needed. Never let self-satisfaction keep you from meeting them. If you do, it is because you are attached to your own views. In Zen, there is no sickness worse than that.

commentary

A Commentary on *Exhortations for Those Who Don't Rouse Doubt*

THE DISEASE OF INTELLECT

It is quite natural for Boshan to begin with the problem of mistaking mere intellectual understanding for realization. Who among us has not made that mistake? The term "wavering mind," which he repeats often, is literally "arising ceasing mind": the restless, samsaric mind of life and death. In the present context, instead of putting the wavering mind to rest, you end up using it to spin intellectual interpretations, a subtle sleight of hand to veil the precipitous doubt underfoot.

See the foolish imitation that results: raising a finger or fist, composing Zen-like poetry without having resolved the great matter, and so on. In some Zen circles nowadays, to declare "Don't know!" has become the same kind of blind imitation—mouthing someone else's words in a way that actually prevents real doubt from arising. As we will see, Boshan repeatedly condemns such "performance Zen." Another critic in the late Ming dynasty, the scholar Qian Qianyi, stated:

Present-day Zen is not Zen. It is no more than beating and shouting...The demonstration in the Dharma hall is like actors ascending the stage; paying homage and offering certification of enlightenment are similar to a drama acted out by little boys... They boast to each other about the number of their followers, the extent of their fame, and the wealth of their profits and patronage.[6]

Is it any better today? Let go of everything you've accumulated over the years, all the pop Zen you've read, your intellectual understanding, and so on, and honestly recognize: I don't really know anything. One drop of this is better than a truckload of borrowed plumage.

Is your zazen firmly established, or is it still something your wavering mind goes into and out of? Are you still detoured from your doubt by intellectual sleight of hand? Be patient, but not lax, properly focused on the matter at hand. Inquire in all sincerity, and with your whole body—not just in your head.

Look at the opening of this enlightenment poem about the sun having always been round—how different is it from your own situation?

Around the seventh year of Xiantong era
(circa 866)

I was born and soon began to inquire into
   the Way.
Wherever I went I met with words
but couldn't understand them.
The doubt block within me
like a large wicker basket.
For three springs I found no joy
even stopping among wooded streams...

Did the author pontificate about the words and phrases, the koans and commentaries he met with everywhere? No, he recognized he couldn't really understand them. Thus, he sincerely searched and was eventually able to have a genuine Dharma encounter, which he details in the climax of his poem:

My doubt block shattered
and fell with a crash!
Raising my head to look about
I saw that the sun has always been round.
After that I stumble along—
step by step.
And ever since then
have been joyful.
Belly now full
having eaten my fill,
I no longer go in search
begging bowl in hand.

The author of this poem was Luohan. His disciple, Fayan, became founder of the Zen school that bears his name. When they met at Luohan's monastery, he asked Fayan why he was not out on pilgrimage. Fayan replied, "I don't know." The master said, "Not knowing is most intimate!" With this, Fayan broke through.

Don't be afraid of really not knowing; it is the entrance. But don't dwell in it either. This is the theme of the second section.

THE DISEASE OF QUIET MEDITATION

Boshan turns to the disease of attachment to quiet meditation. If you think you've gotten beyond the disease of intellectual entanglement, then this will likely shake you from your slumber.

The crux of this exhortation warns against seeking shelter from the storm in the apparently peaceful cave of dead stillness. Is your zazen an escape from problems, within or without? Such is not Zen; it is the death of Zen. Great doubt is not a matter of blotting out our actual problems; it opens us up to them, even as it directs us to their source.

Boshan speaks ill of "Hinayana" attainment. This derogatory term is often used in Zen to refer to anyone attached to self-serving states. It is not a sectarian criticism of non-"Mahayana" ("great vehicle" which saves all) schools of Buddhism. Still, Boshan cannot escape criticism here. I trust he will humbly bow to political correctness.

At any rate, the precious point he makes is that even such profound meditative states can be tempting escapes. Beware! Genuine "just sitting" is enough—if it goes all the way.

If it doesn't, you may end up losing your temper when something intrudes on the peaceful state you've cultivated while sitting. Far from peaceful, your wavering mind ends up more frightened and frustrated than before, becoming what Boshan called demon-possessed. If you are honest with yourself, how can genuine doubt not arise?

Boshan and others emphasize two entrances to this doubt: not knowing where we came from at birth and where we will go at death. Once we open up, however, we realize that we really don't know anything we don't even know where we really are right now. Here great doubt manifests.

Boshan does not go into detail here, but the doubt at first may be vague and unfocused. No problem. With all the wonder and curiosity that you have, open up to the fact that you don't know. In proper and sustained zazen, let this doubt clearly manifest. Driven by the genuine need to know, calmly but constantly inquire. Proceed so that this doubt encompasses all. When this comes to a head, it congeals and solidifies into the doubt block, also called the great doubt block or simply great doubt. This, broken through, is great awakening—body-mind fallen off.

Now, what actually arises in your practice? Present that in a real one-on-one encounter—not what you think should arise. Otherwise, you are likely covering over concerns that are there and need to be acknowledged. This leads to the third section.

THE DISEASE OF SUPPRESSION

These are exhortations or admonishments—stern warnings—and Boshan reaches his stride toward the end of this third section. They must have been relevant for the people around him. I trust they are relevant for you too.

In the present context, discriminating consciousness and karmic consciousness (already mentioned in section one) are basically the same delusion. As long as the delusive nature of all such consciousness—and thus the great matter of life and death—is not decisively broken through, there is a great temptation to try and cut oneself off from it and deny it.

Such suppression doesn't work. The very attempt is an activity of deluded consciousness. No attempt to resolve it within the framework of consciousness will work. On the other hand, in great doubt, the self-experience itself and all activities of consciousness naturally come to an end of their own accord. They are not suppressed.

Hakuin, for example, often described his own experience: "All the workings of mind—thought, consciousness, and emotions—hung suspended." "Ordinary mental processes, consciousness, and emotion all ceased to function."[7] Otherwise, face it: you may be in Zen robes, but you're still whistling Dixie.

About forty years ago my Dharma Granddad Zenkei Shibayama stated:

> Often I come across people who just naively believe that samadhi in art, or no mind in expert skill, is the same as that of Zen because of their superficial resemblance. According to them, there can naturally be dancing Zen, painting Zen, piano-playing Zen, or laboring Zen. This is an extremely careless misunderstanding. They have failed to see the basic difference between Zen and psychological absorption in an art or skill.[8]

There certainly is genuine Zen action. From where does it arise? That is the point. It is not merely a matter of mental state, psychological absorption, or suppression.

A crucial concern for us as we work this out in work, and play, in the world. Alone with a crying baby or a dying loved one—what do you do?

THE DISEASE OF EMPTINESS

Don't get attached, even to emptiness! From the outside, it may sound like nonsense: If there's nothing, how can you be attached? And yet, that's exactly what can happen. Through proper practice and lifestyle, it is fairly easy to get free from most attachments. You can even get quite skillful at it. Then you abide for a while in your pretty little hole, stinking up the place.

This will not do. One real koan, properly applied, will do. Now, what will you do: spend the rest of your life wavering between the plague of endless doubts and the futility of dead emptiness, or once and for all break through your great doubt? Dahui reminds us: "This very lack of anywhere to get a grip is the time to let go of your body and your life."[9]

True inquiry has nothing to do with abiding in mere emptiness, let alone learning to give correct answers to koans. Firm in great trust and motivated by great doubt, in sustained practice, let it all go. Don't even abide in any "emptiness" that remains. Boshan clears the way by sealing off every possible escape.

When the mind-train is going too fast, we want to slow it down. Then the scenery can be seen clearly and in detail, rather than just as a blur. The point, however, is not merely to slow down or calm down mind by temporarily emptying it; it must once come to a full and complete STOP. Then SEE what is there.

In a word, the Chinese Buddhist traditions of Tiantai (Tendai in Japanese) and Chan (or Zen) can be said, in their own way, to condense the rich Indian Buddhist traditions to stopping and seeing. Stopping or samatha: that is, bringing wavering sense-experience itself, including mind, to a full and complete stop. Seeing or vipassana: that is, realizing, actually seeing through, what is there. Not two different approaches or practices, but simply two sides of the same coin: that is, being without self. Mere emptying will not do.

A Japanese Zen master of the thirteenth century known as Mugai Nyodai is said to have awakened when the bottom of the water bucket she was carrying burst. She expressed it in her enlightenment poem as:

> ...No more water in the bucket,
> no more moon in the water—
> emptiness in the palm of my hand!

This fifth section on attachment to speculation is similar to the first one on intellectual attachment. Such a practice can be called "chewing gum Zen": in mouth and mind it tastes good for a moment—we can maybe even blow a couple of bubbles with it—but soon it loses its taste. Or perhaps we might regard it as "cotton candy Zen": it dissolves without satisfying our real hunger.

A number of Zen terms are mentioned here. These expressions were obviously bandied about—chewed on momentarily then summarily spat out—in Boshan's time. For example, "unity attained" is the fifth of Dongshan's *Five Ranks*—a profound poetic expression of Zen by the cofounder of the Sōtō tradition. How tempting to speculate on and dumbly repeat such living expressions! And with it the life is gone. Boshan's attitude toward such speculation and Zen talk is crystal clear.

Tell me, how do you express it here and now? Without resorting to Zen rhetoric, how do you express it?

Once karmic consciousness comes to an end, do all our other entanglements also cease just like that? Let me make it relevant for present purposes: If awakening is total and immediate, why is practice endless? The sun rises at a certain moment, and with it day breaks and all is clearly illumined; the snow and ice, however, take time to break up and melt. A baby is born at a certain moment, though it may take years to walk, talk, and help others.[10]

Similarly, by nature, genuine awakening is immediate, total, and complete. Working it out in this world, in every aspect of our actions, speech, and thought, is another matter. There is practice to rouse and break through great doubt; there is also practice afterward. Don't neglect either one, or confuse one with the other.

Dahui was fond of stating: "Just get to the root, don't worry about the branches." In the present context: Get to the root now; in time the branches will flower. Practice must culminate in awakening—and be endless. How does practice culminate in awakening? And how is it endless? Mere speculation will not do. Wumen, in comments on the first case of his *Gateless Barrier*, stated: "With your whole body, rouse this one doubt block."

THE DISEASE OF SPIRITS

In this section on the disease of believing in spirits, Boshan plays on the believers' fears in order to rouse them to truly practice. Enamored with their speculations, the mental constructs are objectified, turned into something that Boshan calls spirits. Then the believer is possessed, trapped by them in endless confusion.

Today we might not speak of spirits, but the problem remains. As we give ourselves to practice, things can become very clear. Words that had seemed impenetrable, beyond comprehension, are suddenly illumined in a new way. Keep your eye sharp, and your heart and mind open. Don't wrap yourself up in temporary insights or be fooled by mere mind states; when they're gone, you're sure to suffer the consequences. The extraordinary ordinariness of Zen cannot be fathomed by such playing with spirits.

What delusions remain for you? Give yourself fully and see through them now. Then work even harder to disperse any entanglements that remain.

THE DISEASE OF ACTING OUT

Here Boshan refers again to the error of imitating Zen actions. He lashes out at this corruption in later sections as well. Such "performance Zen" must have been rampant—just like today!

In sections six and seven, Boshan mentions:

Body and mind are dependent on the confluence of fleeting conditions. However, within all of this, there is one thing that comes and goes, free in both motion and rest, without form or substance, shining from the sense organs. Spread out, it fills the universe; gathered in, not a dust mote remains!

Eyes see, ears hear, the tongue speaks, the nose smells odors, hands grasp, feet run. All this is the true nature of the spiritual self!

Such statements must have been popular at the time, and Boshan criticizes them severely. However, they seem to have been cobbled together from statements found in classic Zen texts, such as *The Record of Linji*—the recorded sayings of the father of Rinzai Zen:

Followers of the Way, mind is without form and pervades the ten directions.

"In the eye it is called seeing, in the ear it is called hearing. In the nose it smells odors, in the mouth it holds converse. In the hands it grasps and seizes, in the feet it runs and carries." Fundamentally it is one pure radiance; divided it becomes the six harmoniously united spheres of sense. If the mind is void, wherever you are, you are emancipated.

Followers of the Way, if you wish to be Dharma, just have no doubts. "Spread out, it fills the entire Dharma realm; gathered in, the smallest hair cannot stand upon it." Distinctly and radiantly shining alone, it has never lacked anything.[11]

Where is the difference? Do you seek it in the words? Do you seek it in action? Or do you seek it in some spiritual self? Either way, you're no better off than the ones Boshan is chastising!

THE DISEASE OF ASCETICISM

Such practices may help purify and prepare, but they should not be mistaken for the Way. Even such noble acts can be corrupted by ego-self—yes, sitting in meditation as well. Obsession with perfecting meditative technique is a common mistake here.

Needless to say, it will not do to prematurely abandon such practices for "anything goes" self-indulgence either, as the last two sections below will show. "Obsessed with a goal (such as enlightenment), preoccupied with achieving liberation" is also not the Way—as Boshan states in the opening of this section.

This is true of great doubt as well:

> These eyeless priests tell practitioners that unless they can raise a great doubt block and then break through it, there can't be any progress in Zen. Instead of teaching them to live by the unborn Buddha mind, they start by forcing them to raise this doubt block any way they can. People who don't have a doubt are now saddled with one. They've turned their Buddha minds into doubt blocks. It's absolutely wrong.[12]

What Bankei criticizes here is not great doubt at all. It's great doubt gone awry—turned into a goal that the self then tries to achieve. Great doubt and great awakening are right under your own feet! Thus Boshan ends this section not with some superhuman, ascetic feat, but rather with the humble, everyday act of clearing away ash. See for yourself: with eyes open, there's not a thing to achieve or to let go. Great doubt, not to mention great awakening—as well as Bankei's "teaching them to live by the unborn Buddha mind"—all are like last night's dream.

THE DISEASE OF SELF-INDULGENCE

In this section, Boshan chillingly portrays those who try to deny their disease by indulging in pathetic antics, parading around as accomplished men and women. Sobering words for all of us.

Such Zen antics stink to high heaven; they are not worth further criticism. Sustained practice, on the other hand, is precious indeed. And yet, real practice is not something we sometimes do—for example, during an intensive retreat or in daily practice. To be what it really is, it must become what we are. Then it is naturally forgotten.

THE DISEASE OF PUTTING ON AIRS

In this final section, Boshan continues with examples of "costume Zen," its excesses and shortcomings.

It can be a great temptation today as well to go off alone into nature and practice free of artificial restrictions. But unless your determination is solid and clear, you will likely go astray.

Three essentials are commonly mentioned for Zen practice: great trust, great determination, and great doubt. For our purposes, I think a proper presentation of great trust and great doubt is enough. Great determination can too easily turn into misguided and destructive willpower, as Boshan suggests in his discussion on the disease of asceticism. Chinese Zen master Gaofeng Yuanmiao of the thirteenth century likened great determination to "the passion that possesses you when, on meeting the enemy who slew your father, you instantly want to cut him in two with your sword."[13]

The end of this passage underlines the value of practice together, supporting and being supported by each other. The final line warns us to beware of dangers. The term here translated as "beware" is the same Chinese character for "Exhortations" in the title. Boshan ends by reminding us to exhort or admonish ourselves.

If your doubt is real, far from interfering with your daily life, it will be just what is needed. Embracing your own doubt, you can open up to others, make room for them, and respond directly to their real needs. In this way, relations with others can be transformed. Here, the Zen Buddhist tradition—I include myself as one poor representative—still has much room to learn and grow.

A Commentary on *Exhortations for Those Who Rouse Doubt*

The opening sentence is repeated in all of these exhortations. What is the meaning of the Sanskrit term *dharmakāya*? Very simply, *dharma* refers to living truth, and *kāya* means body. "Dharma body" has become a kind of metaphysical reality in Buddhist doctrine. In Zen, however, it is embodied Dharma—truth embodied. Not the mere concept or idea, but the living fact itself, concrete and actual. This is what Zen practice and one-on-one are all about. It will become clearer as we go through these exhortations and you apply it in your practice.

Once great doubt has been raised, then the preconceptions, mental fixations, and other delusions, or "fixed views" as they are called in Buddhism, start to unravel. All that we think we know, all that we think we are, falls into doubt.

In proper and sustained practice, it does not take long to experience this great undoing. Once this great doubt settles and matures, you naturally accord with dharmakāya, as Boshan calls it. What is this preliminary experience like? As you may have already experienced, and as Boshan describes here, all is bright and clear, and the delusion of separation is gone. There is no hindrance whatsoever, within or without. And it is directly experienced as such. It is embodied, not conceived or imagined by the self.

In the act of trying to take control of the dharmakāya, however, our clinging to it prevents the life root from being cut off. In the idiom of the American astronaut, we have lift off, but we have yet to return home: "Houston, we have a problem." Once the mind wheel starts churning again, dharmakāya is distorted into a world that I possess and others must conform to. This is no longer dharmakāya, but a pale reflection of it in the mirror of self-delusion. This happens when practice is not thoroughgoing.

If this entrance into great doubt is turned into something and clung to, even the temporary experience of the dissolution of all hindrances gets corrupted. Clinging to it like this, the life root remains. This life root feeds our disease. Disease is inevitable as long as this basic volitional clinging or desire to be—even to be enlightened—exists.

Just a moment ago, not a hint of hindrance could be found anywhere. Now our very body and mind are a painful hindrance. In each of these exhortations Boshan impales us with this statement about being sick through and through—this is not Zen. Don't mistake profound experiences of oneness for awakening!

"Let go on the edge of the precipice and accept what comes! Finish dying, then come back to life and you can no longer be deceived." This is the life root decisively cut off, coming to its own end. This needed turnaround, this transformation or inner revolution, is the heart of Zen: when we have finished dying, then we can really come back to life. Otherwise, we may indulge and delight in temporary experiences where all delusion is gone. But then self-delusion comes back with a vengeance; we may even think we're the biggest no-self around!

Boshan warns us severely, yet also states that it's not difficult. Give yourself to proper practice with good Dharma friends and teachers, and then you'll see that it really is the most simple and natural thing in the world.

The "thrust to your weak point" or blind spot mentioned at the end is like the trigger point for Shiatsu: pressing it, there may be pain. But the point is that once it is properly pressed, the painful delusion is released.

SECOND EXHORTATION

In the first exhortation, Boshan spoke of the world as radiant and without any hindrance. Here is a more dramatic image of all gathered into a whirling vortex. Wavering, wandering mind is impossible here and you feel incredible vitality. Sleep? Who needs it! Food? Ha!

Boshan repeats a similar pattern of first arousing doubt and according with dharmakāya, but then falling under its spell and tripping over your own feet in the process. If these warnings don't seem relevant now, they soon will.

You're like a guard for precious treasure: it's right under your greedy nose, but it's not yours. Again, Boshan offers guidance: "In this state, just throw yourself into it with no regard for danger." Well, have some regard for danger. By all means, throw yourself into it, but please do so with great care. You do need to give yourself fully, but don't be careless or foolish.

Tiantong, also known as Hongzhi Zhengjue, was one of the leading Sōtō masters of the Sung dynasty. Here Tiantong suggests that if one's seeking mind really has come to rest, wherever you turn you're satisfied—your belly is full! It's amazing how many Zen expressions involve food. Does your stomach tell you why?

Richard DeMartino introduced me to Zen Buddhism in the early 1970s at Temple University in Philadelphia. Over fifty years ago he lived in Kyoto. Once he was invited to a celebration at the Rinzai monastery of Nanzenji. Zenkei Shibayama was the head abbot and Zen master training the monks. During the feast, DeMartino was seated next to Shibayama. Japanese sake or rice wine was also available for the guests, so DeMartino offered a cup to Shibayama.

The Zen master politely declined, patting his stomach and saying, in Japanese: "No thank you. My belly's already full."

DeMartino replied: "But you're supposed to be empty."

Shibayama shot back: "Even when I'm full, I'm empty."

Tiantong said, in effect: "Even when I'm empty, I'm full." Is this the same or different?

Boshan seals his second exhortation by warning those with some degree of realization to see their blind spot and be willing to learn from others. As you find all separation dissolving and things illumined like never before, it is essential to clearly see what remains and to apply yourself there.

THIRD EXHORTATION

In the first lines of this exhortation, Boshan is paraphrasing part of a famous Chinese Zen expression of Qingyuan:

> Before I started practicing, mountains were mountains and rivers were rivers; when I had made progress, mountains were not mountains and rivers were not rivers; now that I've come to rest, mountains are mountains and rivers are rivers.

The first stage is that of common sense and ordinary knowledge: I know who I am! The second, which Boshan paraphrases here, describes great doubt. That's when a mountain is not a mountain. The third and final stage sounds identical to the first. What's the difference?

Even if you rouse great doubt, if discursive mind returns you are lost. You're neither here nor there: you're not where you began, but you definitely have not come home, nor come to the end, either. You're stuck somewhere in between. You've yet to arrive here. This is the value of thoroughgoing practice and proper guidance.

I take issue with Boshan's "back in the good old days" rhetoric in this passage. Nowadays, we are so full of intellectual knowledge and our discursive mind runs wild, so, in some ways, it was simpler back then. But we're also at a great advantage: various traditions and teachings are available like never before. Used wisely, they can be of great benefit. Used unwisely, we can get confused and lost. And so could the ancients: there are plenty of examples of them being just as confused and lost as people today.

Don't be fooled by Boshan and his pretentious talk of the ancients! Eventually, it will be recognized that the golden age of Zen in the modern world is beginning now. We are very fortunate. "These are the good old days," as Master Carly Simon sings.

Boshan wrote in this passage that not even a trace of satori remains yet precisely here you need to encounter someone who really knows. If you don't see why, beware!

In his introduction, Boshan summarizes and clarifies this initial process of rousing great doubt:

> A person intent on practicing Zen doesn't see sky above or ground below, doesn't see mountains as mountains or rivers as rivers, walks and sits without knowing. Among a huge crowd, he sees no one. His whole self, inside and out, solidifies into one doubt block and the whole world seems as if drawn into a vortex. Vow never to stop until this doubt block has been broken through. This is the essential point of practice.

Boshan is clearly describing and hammering away at the danger of falling into dead stillness, of abiding in emptiness and getting stuck there. He has already addressed these sicknesses in sections two and four of *Exhortations for Those Who Don't Rouse Doubt.* Now he's challenging those who have begun the real work, then gone astray.

Shishuang Qingzhu was an early Chinese Zen master in the tradition of "silent illumination." The reference to him and to dying seated in meditation is found in Case 96 of the Sōtō Zen koan anthology *The Book of Serenity.* After Master Shishuang passed away, the master's former attendant asked the senior monk about their master's teaching. Shishuang had used expressions like: "Cease and desist all activity of the senses," "Ten thousand years in one moment of thought"—mentioned at the beginning of this section—"Be cold ash, a dead tree," "Be an old incense burner in an ancient shrine," "Be a strip of pure white silk." The senior monk replied that they illustrate oneness, that is, equality without differentiation. The attendant responded that in that case the senior monk does not understand their late teacher. The senior monk then told the attendant to bring incense. "If I do not understand our master's teaching," the senior monk declared, "then I will not be able to die before the incense burns out." Sure enough, before the incense burned out, the senior monk died sitting in zazen. But the point of the case is what comes next: the attendant then taps the now dead senior monk on his shoulder and concludes: "Well, as far as dying seated in meditation or while standing, you are not lacking. But concerning our master's teaching, you haven't seen it even in a dream!"

I trust you can discern, from your own experience, the crucial point that the senior monk had missed with his empty oneness. It was fatal. As a koan case it dramatically—and literally—reveals the danger of dead sitting, and shows that the Zen tradition has been struggling with this since early on. Note that Boshan mentions there were plenty like this in Shishuang's monastery back in the ninth century.

If we get stuck in our sitting through, even at that profoundly unified state of great doubt, it is as if we are dead. Thus Boshan exhorts us to take that further step so that we can spring back to life and function freely.

Boshan again quotes the renowned Sōtō master Tiantong. The stock image is of a carp working its way upriver, then taking a final leap to be transformed into a dragon. This final leap has nothing to do with words and phrases, nor with sitting—even with sitting through.

As mentioned, dharmakāya means embodied Dharma, living truth. Though the initial act of coming into accord may not be easy, ultimately it's very simple. Once great doubt naturally arises, self-delusion starts to come undone. The delusion that you are unravels, and you embody the living truth, inseparable. This is the entrance to the Way. It's not about mere understanding, states of mind, or experiences.

This is not a state; when you become attached to it, however, you turn it into one. Boshan is not theorizing, so his words can be confusing if you don't have the eye. At first, he speaks positively of dharmakāya. However, he continues by writing negatively about it as a state, because if it is grasped, this is what it becomes. So I added "what you take to be" in my translation. Whether you dwell in the joy of your attainment or suffer in the dissatisfaction of your un-attainment, they are both delusive states. One has a little more glitter, that's all.

Boshan, by way of Dongshan, invokes the crane as a symbol of longevity, but it does not abide. Likewise, the phoenix is a symbol of awakening, but it does not reside. Finish dying; then fully return to life! That is what it refers to. Then there's no place to get stuck—

no place to abide or reside. There's not even a trace of "enlightenment."

The language used to express it is intimately connected with what is expressed. Zen is not attached or limited to words. And yet, properly expressed, language can be a great aid, can't it? Throughout this book, I have offered many examples. Chew on them, digest them, and then you can eliminate them. Hakuin wrote:

> Don't try to tell me my poems are too
>   hard—
> Face it, the problem is your own eyeless
>   state
> When you come to a word you don't under-
>   stand, quick
> Bite it at once! Chew it right to the pith!
> Once you're soaked to the bone in death's
>   cold sweat,
> All the koans Zen has are yanked up, root
>   and stem.[14]

Don't get stuck inside, or outside, the "bucket of lacquer"—that is, the remaining ignorance and delusions.

The first paragraph depicts what can happen when willful striving remains: a self-fulfilling delusion is created and mistaken for the real thing. The second paragraph expresses the real thing: what we are is none other than what is.

The sickness talked about in this exhortation is a very general term for any hindrance or delusion along the way, anything short of full and complete awakening. This term is used in many different senses and contexts, so beware in your reading. Attachment to the seated posture is sometimes called a Zen sickness. Whatever it is, if we grasp after it and turn it into something, even the noble and lofty can turn into a disease—beware!

"Innumerable sicknesses are found in the dharma-kāya. Fatally succumb once to this—only then will you realize the root of the disease." This is why it is important not to just sit, but to sit through. Boshan mentions three sicknesses, but there are various lists. One borrows from the ox-herding pictures: The first sickness is to look for the ox while riding it. The second is to realize the ox but refuse to get off it. The third is to penetrate further but not realize total liberation.

Boshan ends: "This does not, of course, apply to the

blind, deaf, and dumb." Is he criticizing the hopelessly ignorant, or praising those who are free of sense attachment? Best to read this Zen stuff without using your eyes.

How do we practice so as to open up to these experiences as genuine pointers, without getting stuck in them? The natural first step is to give ourselves to the practice so that we can confirm this opening right under our own feet, to see that the whole self-centered world that we create is a delusion. Then, naturally, let the delusion go. Everything that we thought we knew, everything that we thought we were, falls into marvelous, liberating great doubt.

Reality is marvelous and liberating. But if self-craving remains it can seem frightening and unsettling, for what I identify as myself is seen through for what it is. This is very good and true and real—but you've got to let go!

Great doubt is right underfoot. In more traditional Buddhist phrasing: it is good, it is proper, and it is correct to doubt what should be doubted and to examine whether it is real or not. Delusions deserve to be doubted. If they are not doubted, they maintain their hold on us and we continue to suffer. Through proper practice, the single saucer lamp in the room, as it's called, clearly and naturally brings to light our delusion—the delusion that we are.

> In India and China, in the past and the present, of all the worthies who spread this light, none did anything more than simply resolve this one doubt. The thousand doubts, the ten thousand doubts are just this one doubt. Resolve this doubt and no doubt remains.

You don't need to blindly believe—even the Buddhist teachings. You don't need to blindly follow—even a so-called teacher. That is genuine Zen Buddhism. Let great doubt that is underfoot, that you are, be what it is. There is no greater trust or faith. Let that be your Way.

Why wait for another earthquake, tsunami, or other crisis or tragedy, internal or external, to reveal that the ground underfoot is not as firm and solid as you think? Let great doubt open underfoot: Who is this one who knows exactly what I'm saying? Who is this one who has no idea? Who is this one who wants more than anything to help, but ends up hurting instead? Who is behind it all? Illumine that and the essential work is done. Then the single saucer lamp is quite enough. For it reveals that there really are no delusions, there is no place for them to even arise. Don't just follow my words; confirm it in your bones.

Buddhism speaks of *samsara*, *dukkha*, the great matter of life and death (or birth and death), and so on. Such terms are another way of referring to the great doubt that has yet to be seen through. As Boshan stated in the quotation from his introduction: "Eventually you will break through this doubt block and realize what a worthless notion life and death is—ha!" It is not a speculative or abstract concern: this I, this me that has come into being and will one day cease—what is that?

SEVENTH EXHORTATION

The dharmakāya is truth embodied—living truth. In other words, when you realize what things really are, when the barriers fall away, you are in accord with and not separate from the dharmakāya. Then indeed the whole world is your eye, clear and simple. The whole world is just this! The mental world that we create dissolves into just this!

The expressions in the first paragraph, stating that the whole world is the monk's eye and so forth, may sound bombastic. As a poetic way of expressing the falling away of delusions and the realization of what is right in front of our face, however, they are quite natural and to the point.

The second and third paragraphs show what happens when we don't go all the way through. In the final paragraph, Boshan uses the dramatic image of turning somersaults on the edge of a cliff, then simply doing what needs to be done. Turning somersaults here is comparable to the image in the fourth exhortation, where Boshan quotes Tiantong: "Just cutting off the ten directions in sitting, the fish falls short of the Dragon Gate." Leaping through this gate, the carp transforms into a dragon in the same way that one turns somersaults on the edge of a cliff, then goes about one's business. This final leap is essential. However, it cannot be done by self-will; self-will is what keeps us chained down. This leap can happen once that dissolves.

EIGHTH EXHORTATION

Boshan warns us not to get wrapped up in profound states of serene clarity, but instead to turn around and take one more step, thus to return to the world with open arms, to "enter the market with open hands"—as the title for a poem on the tenth ox-herding picture puts it. Boshan then scolds us for refusing to meet with Dharma friends and warns us that even in a state of great purity, delusions can still arise. This point is taken up in the next section.

Boshan quotes Tiantong again, whom he quoted also in sections two and four. Tiantong is one of the great Chinese Sōtō Zen masters active about fifty years before the time of Dōgen.

The final paragraph points the way through. The

final sentence reeks of violence, though I take it as encouragement to destroy such delusions within.

This eighth exhortation challenges us to leap out of the apparently free and open space we find ourselves in. How do you respond?

NINTH EXHORTATION

With psychological insight, Boshan describes and warns us of magical visions and the like that may appear. He naturally uses metaphors and figures of speech that just as naturally sound bizarre to us today—unless you grew up in the 1960s as I did!

I trust you can see what he is getting at, though. If not, don't worry about it. Maybe tomorrow or somewhere down the line you'll find yourself saying: "So this is what Boshan was talking about!"

The *Surangama Sutra* is one of the leading Mahayana sutras also important in the Zen tradition. The *Sutra on the Contemplation of Immeasurable Life* is central to the Pure Land faith.

Boshan kindly explains here that even though one sees through the emptiness of all things, if attachment remains, then delusions will appear. He uses a term for demons; today we might speak of it as subjective or unconscious delusions, mental obsessions, and so on. Indeed, greedily seeking after enlightenment does more harm than good if we lack the proper foundation in mind and body.

The old monk's so-called blindness and deafness is far from misfortune. It is truly seeing through. Is there still pain, sleepiness, mental scattering for you? Stable and settled in sustained practice, they become mulch, fuel for the fire. Then nothing can really get in the way. Even misfortune.

TENTH EXHORTATION

In the first paragraph, the unity of reality and appearance is a technical phrase used in Dongshan's *Five Ranks*. But that need not concern us here. The point, as Boshan makes clear, is that the life root is cut off—instead of prematurely letting go of the doubt. The difference is decisive.

Any word that dislodges delusion and prompts the needed turnaround at that time and place is a "living word." "The fire god seeks fire" were dead words for three years when the monk held on to them; those very same words became living words once his great doubt was roused.[15] These words are also called turning words. It doesn't even have to be a word. It could be anything, although in the developed Zen tradition, it often was a loaded word or phrase that sparked realization. In that sense, it is a turnaround, a revolution, a revelation if you like.

The fault is in turning round too soon. Instead, a living word can be used to truly turn round. Don't just mimic Zenistic expressions or you'll suck the life out of them! And never be in a hurry to save others while your own eye is clouded.

The final paragraph sums up well the *Exhortations*, and the essence of genuine Zen practice. Take great care to naturally rouse your doubt into a massive doubt block so that it breaks up on its own accord. Anything less is in vain. Once it breaks up, the true dignity of each and every one is revealed; beauty beyond compare is manifest everywhere.

Then you'll know what needs to be done in this world. You'll not always succeed; I often fail. But you'll know what needs to be done, and you'll be able to give all to it and learn in the process. Others will not always understand; the desired result may not come. But that, too, will be the Dharma in its fullness.

Acknowledgments

My thanks go to Richard Jaffe of Duke University for urging me to send my manuscripts to Wisdom, and to my editor Andy Francis, who recognized the need for it to be published. Chang Chen-chi published an English translation of excerpts from Boshan's *Exhortations* back in 1959 in *The Practice of Zen* (pp. 72–79) More recently (2006), Sheng Yen's *Attaining the Way: A Guide to the Practice of Chan Buddhism* included excerpts translated by Guo Gu (Jimmy Yu) (pp. 19–22). The present complete translation would not have been possible without the great assistance of my colleague Kenji Kinugawa at Hanazono University. Colleagues and scholar-monks Zenkei Noguchi, Eirei Yoshida, and Takuma Senda at Hanazono University, Julianna Lipschutz of the University of Pennsylvania's East Asian Collection, and Haochen (Jerry Yu) of the University of Zurich also offered valuable comment. Unless cited in the endnotes, translations are mine; any mistakes are my own. I look forward to frank feedback from readers. Titles for the first set of exhortations have been added for ease of understanding; there are no titles in the original text. For the Chinese-Japanese texts quoted and other technical materials, see *Zen Classics for the Modern World* (Philadelphia: Diane Publishing, 2011), or the retreat transcripts at the website beingwithoutself.org.

Notes

1. Yampolsky 1971, 144 revised.
2. Waddell 1984, 129–30 revised.
3. Buswell 1988, 373 revised.
4. Yampolsky 1971, 146 revised.
5. Cleary 1977, 38–39 revised.
6. Wu 2008, 159–60 revised.
7. Yoshizawa 2009, 250; Waddell 2009, 25.
8. Shibayama 1974, 75 revised.
9. Cleary 1977, 12 revised.
10. See Broughton 2009, 153.
11. Sasaki 2009, 165 and 287 revised.
12. Waddell 1984, 57 revised.
13. Miura and Sasaki 1966, 246.
14. Waddell 1996, 84 revised.
15. See Shore 2008, 115 and 202.

Bibliography

Broughton, Jeffrey Lyle. *Zongmi on Chan*. New York: Columbia University Press, 2009.

Buswell, Robert E., Jr. "The 'Short-cut' Approach of *K'an-hua* Meditation" in *Sudden and Gradual: Approaches to Enlightenment in Chinese Thought*, edited by Peter N. Gregory. Honolulu: University of Hawaii Press, 1988.

Cleary, Christopher, translator. *Swampland Flowers: The Letters and Lectures of Zen Master Ta Hui*. New York: Grove Press, 1977.

Miura, Isshū, and Ruth Fuller Sasaki. *Zen Dust: The History of the Koan and Koan Study in Rinzai (Lin-chi) Zen*. New York: Harcourt, Brace & World, 1966.

Sasaki, Ruth Fuller, translator. *The Record of Linji*. Honolulu: University of Hawaii Press, 2009.

Shibayama, Zenkei. *Zen Comments on the Mumonkan*. New York: Harper & Row, 1974.

Shore, Jeff. *Being Without Self: Zen for the Modern World*. Rotterdam: Asoka, 2008.

Waddell, Norman, translator. *The Unborn: The Life and Teaching of Zen Master Bankei*. San Francisco: North Point Press, 1984.

———. *The Essential Teachings of Zen Master Hakuin.* Boston: Shambhala, 1994.

———. *Hakuin's Precious Mirror Cave.* Berkeley: Counterpoint, 2009.

———. translator. *Zen Words for the Heart: Hakuin's Commentary on the Heart Sutra.* Boston: Shambhala, 1996

Wu, Jiang. *Enlightenment in Dispute: The Reinvention of Chan Buddhism in Seventeenth-Century China.* New York: Oxford University Press, 2008.

Yampolsky, Philip B., translator. *The Zen Master Hakuin: Selected Writings.* New York: Columbia University Press, 1971.

Yoshizawa, Katsuhiro. *The Religious Art of Zen Master Hakuin.* Berkeley: Counterpoint, 2009.

Index

About the Author

 Jeff Shore (1953) was born in Philadelphia, USA. After ten years studying and practicing in the United States, he went to Japan in 1981. He first spent a year living with Mumon Yamada, head abbot of Myoshinji monastery in Kyoto, and got his toes wet training at the monastery of Shofukuji in Kobe. In 1982 he began practice under Zenkei Shibayama's successor, Keido Fukushima, then Zen master and later head abbot of the major Rinzai complex of Tofukuji in Kyoto. He spent the next twenty-five years in rigorous Zen training there, completed the training, and became Fukushima Roshi's lay successor. Jeff's focus is directly pointing out the very core of Zen and the heart of living Buddhism. Jeff is also professor of Zen in the Modern World at Hanazono University in Kyoto, the sole Rinzai-affiliated university in the world, where he has taught since 1987. He is a husband and a father. He lives in Kyoto where he also has a small place—the Rokoan hermitage—open for those who want to deepen their practice. Jeff leads retreats worldwide.

Also Available
from Wisdom Publications

THE CEASING OF NOTIONS
An Early Zen Text from the Dunhuang Caves
with Selected Comments
Soko Morinaga
Introduced by Martin Collcutt

"This powerful little book is a jewel of Zen Buddhism. Roshi Soko Morinaga goes right to the point of practice and realization."—Joan Halifax, founding abbot, Upaya Zen Center

THE GATELESS GATE
The Classic Book of Zen Koans
Kōun Yamada
Foreword by Ruben L. F. Habito

"Yamada Roshi's straightforward commentary on the Wu-men kuan (Mumonkan) is again available in this new edition, and I'm delighted."—Robert Aitken, author of *Taking the Path of Zen*

DONGSHAN'S FIVE RANKS
Keys to Enlightenment
Ross Bolleter

"Very well done."—Robert Aitken

ZEN
The Authentic Gate
Kōun Yamada
Foreword by David R. Loy

"Yamada's introduction to Zen is a welcome and dense primer that has much to offer novices as well as experienced practitioners."—*Publishers Weekly*

THE ART OF JUST SITTING
Essential Writings on the Zen Practice of Shikantaza
Edited by John Daido Loori
Introduced by Taigen Dan Leighton

"The single most comprehensive treasury of writings on the subject in English."—John Daishin Buksbazen, author of *Zen Meditation in Plain English*

THE ZEN TEACHING OF HOMELESS KODO
Shohaku Okumura and Kosho Uchiyama
Edited by Molly Delight Whitehead

"Kodo Sawaki was straight-to-the-point, irreverent, and deeply insightful—and one of the most influential Zen teachers for us in the West. I'm very happy to see this book."—Brad Warner, author of *Hardcore Zen*

About Wisdom Publications

Wisdom Publications is the leading publisher of classic and contemporary Buddhist books and practical works on mindfulness. To learn more about us or to explore our other books, please visit our website at wisdompubs.org or contact us at the address below.

Wisdom Publications
199 Elm Street
Somerville, MA 02144 USA

We are a 501(c)(3) organization, and donations in support of our mission are tax deductible.

Wisdom Publications is affiliated with the Foundation for the Preservation of the Mahayana Tradition (FPMT).

31901059712986